Growing Readers

Thoughts and Feelings

Thoughts and Feelings

Sad

Written by Sylvia Root Tester
Photos by David M. Budd

The Child's World®, Inc.

Published by The Child's World®, Inc.

Design and Production:
The Creative Spark, San Juan Capistrano, CA

Photos: © 1998 David M. Budd Photography

Library of Congress Cataloging-in-Publication Data

Tester, Sylvia Root, 1939–
     Sad / by Sylvia Root Tester.
          p. cm. — (Thoughts and feelings)
     Summary: Simple rhyming text describes sadness, how it feels, and
what can cause it.
     ISBN 1-56766-673-6 (lib. bdg : alk. paper)
     1. Sadness in children—Juvenile literature. [1. Sadness.] I. Title. II. Series.
BF723.S15T47   1999
152.4—dc21
                                                                          99-25378
                                                                          CIP

It's hard to keep going when you feel bad,

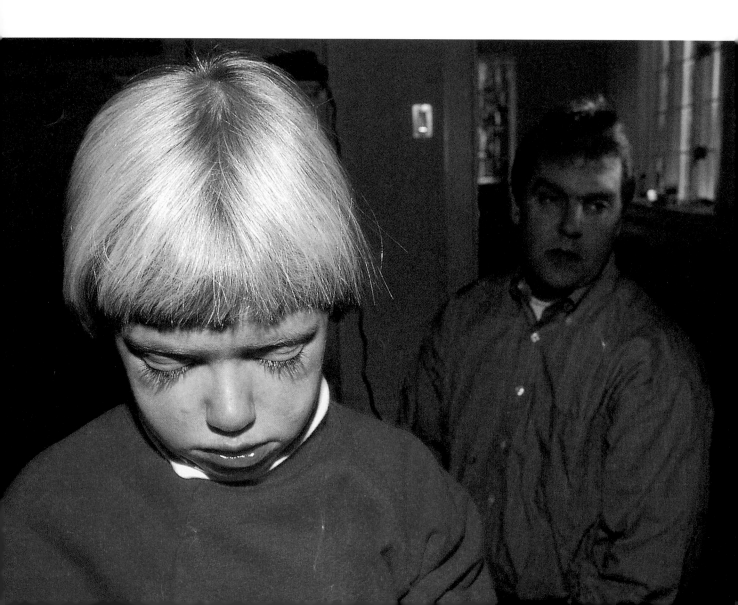

and today, all day long,
I've been feeling sad.

You see, Mr. Chips died.
He got sick Saturday.
Oh, I hated to see him
feeling that way.

It made me so

SAD.

It hurt me so!

We were going to Grandma's,
but Mr. Chips couldn't go!
Why, he couldn't even go
along for the ride.
I had to leave him on his
bed inside.

Dad took him to the vet
while I was away.
He died, and they buried
him that same day.

Dad told me later.

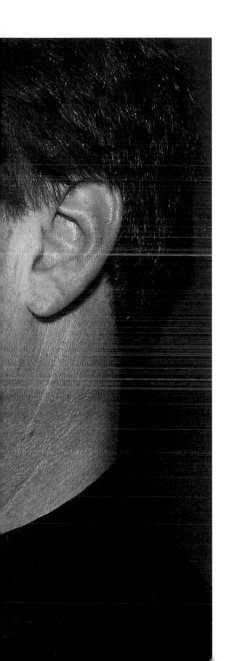

That's when I cried.
I wanted to find
a good place to hide.

17

Mom says it's OK
to feel that bad.
Everyone does sometimes.

20

Everyone feels sad when friends are hurt...

or move away...

when people die...

or they have
a bad day...

or when good friends fight.

When these things happen,
people don't feel right.

When sad things happen,
there's one thing to do...
Find someone who will
comfort you.

For Further Information and Reading

Books

Berry, Joy Wilt. *Feeling Sad.* New York: Scholastic Trade, 1996.

Mundy, Michaelene. *Sad Isn't Bad.* St. Meinrad, IN: Abbey Press, 1998.

Web Sites

Why Am I So Sad?
http://www.kidshealth.org/kid/feeling/sadness.html

What If Someone I love Dies?
http://www.kidshealth.org/kid/feeling/somedie.html

Kid's Guide to Divorce:
http://www.kidshealth.org/kid/feeling/divorce.html

We're Moving: http://www.kidshealth.org/kid/feeling/moving.html

Coping with Separation:
http://www.cts.com/crash/habtsmrt/ppp.html

Fairy tales and stories about thoughts and feelings from
all over the world: http://www.familyinternet.com/StoryGrowby/